NIGHT (

By Bill Stenson

CW00395013

Published for the author by Inscribe Media Limited, of Darlington

First published in the United Kingdom in 2004 on behalf of the author by Inscribe Media, of Darlington

ISBN 0-9523341-9-4

A proportion of the profits from this book will be divided between Cancer Research UK and the Alzheimer's Society

ACKNOWLEDGEMENT

Many thanks to my wife Laura
for all her loyal support down the years
and to my secretary Pauline Raine
for typing the manuscript over many hours.

Bill Stenson

*To Daisy & Dell -
Best Wishes, Bill Stenson*

CHAPTER ONE

The story begins in the village of Ovington, known as the Maypole Village, in the North Riding of Yorkshire. This is where I was born, poor and one of a large family. Mother and father were 'the salt of the earth'. They had ten children, but two were lost at birth, stillborn I think. It was the norm in those days to have big families and ours was no exception.

My father was a stonemason. My mother was raised in St. Cuthbert's orphanage having lost her parents in America. What a hard life she had bringing up eight of us on poor wages, but we never went short of food. We had a plain diet with plenty of vegetables, good rabbit pie, fish from the river etc. If we had a cold, mother would rub goose grease on our chests covered with brown paper. It either killed or cured you! I used to object strongly, but still I had to have the treatment! We usually had a goose at Christmas and always had a supply of goose grease which mother put into jars. When my father worked for Mr Peat, the MP at Wyciffe Hall, we lived on the River Tees at Wycliffe and father would gaff the salmon as they swam upriver to spawn.

I was christened in Wycliffe Church, a beautiful church set near to the river and in a small hamlet. I have since been back and nothing has changed very much apart from the alterations which residents have made to their houses. They call it progress.

We lived next door to the Blacksmith shop in Ovington. If the blacksmith had any horses that he wasn't going to shoe straight away he would tie them to our fence. Mother told him on many occasions to move them as they were damaging the fence. Then one day after many a row with him, the horses were eating the flowers and grass in the little garden and she untied them and chased them on to the Green. There was a right old row between my mother and the very irate blacksmith, but it did stop him and it was only on very rare occasions that mother would allow him to tie them up. Many farms had a flat rulley, which was pulled by a horse. I have a photo taken on a rulley at The Four Halls when I was young. It must have been a very hot summer because I looked really tanned.

School was not a happy place for me. When I first went to Wycliffe School which was a Roman Catholic School, those pupils who weren't of the Catholic religion were made to wait in the play area until morning assembly and prayers were over. If it was wet we had to go into the toilets to wait, or stand under the canopy. It was not a good beginning for a young lad. This only lasted for a year or two, but I never forgot it. I could not speak properly until I was about seven years old. I had a stutter, which was not helped by the corporal punishment given out by the schoolteachers as was normal in those days.

When I moved on to junior school I was forever playing truant. As soon as I heard the hounds after the fox I, and one or two more boys, would go off to follow them. Needless to say we got the cane the next morning. One day my mother was confronted by one of the residents who was blaming my brothers and I for pinching apples. My mother, who was carrying a pail of water from the village pump at the time, told him in no uncertain terms that we were not the guilty parties. He kept on insisting it was us, until mother eventually lost her temper, threw the water over him, slammed the pail over his head and sent him packing!

When I was around 11 years old we moved to Forcett, a small village in the North Riding of Yorkshire. I attended the village school, a walk of about one mile. It was during the war and we were all issued with gas masks. Everybody hated them, including the evacuees who stayed in the surrounding villages. In the Forties we also had the Land Army girls and some Italian prisoners-of-war who worked on the farms.

My stutter improved later at around the age of about 12 - until the day the headmaster gave me a walloping. He had informed the class that anyone getting a particular sum right would be allowed to leave early. This had never happened to me, ever! My brother, who was in the same classroom, flicked the answer over to me and I put up my hand to say that I knew the answer, much to the surprise of the headmaster. I answered the question and he then asked me to do the sum on the blackboard. I just could not do it! He accused me of looking in the answer book. I told him that I had not. I did not want to get my brother into trouble. He took his stick and started lacing into me - across my shoulders and on my hands. This went on for some time until I fell to the floor in pain. I got up and kicked him on his shins. By this time my brother had come to my aid with a teacher from the next class to stop him. I told him I would tell my father when I got home. When my father saw the weals and bruises, he went berserk and wasted no time in going to the Headmaster's house to 'sort him out'. What he said to him, I have no idea, but he never touched me again and it was said that my father gave him a good hiding. It was to be a few years later when my brother and I got our own back.

Life was hard for my father. During the time he spent on the dole he cycled as far as Stockton to look for work, but to no avail. That's how tough it was in the thirties. Then came the war in 1939 and work got better for stonemasons.

I can vaguely remember a Lancaster Bomber being shot down near Caldwell. We got on our bikes and raced to where we could see the smoke. When we got there we waited around inquisitively and were told to 'clear off' when the rear gunner was brought out. He was covered in blood. When I saw him I fainted and they had to attend to me. We were quite close and the ammunition was going off, bullets were exploding and the plane was burning. I am not quite sure if they got all of the airmen out or not. We hoped they would be alive. My mother gave me a good 'telling off' for going to the crash site, but I would not have missed it for all the world. There was also the occasion when I saw a German Messerschmidt shot down at Forcett by a Spitfire during September of 1941. The plane came down at Whorlton: the pilot baled out and was taken prisoner by the villagers.

We also had refugees staying in the villages around the North-East. We weren't able to take in many because we already had too many mouths to feed, but they were made very welcome. My father still found work very hard to get and worked for the local quarry, building shelters for the quarry men to take cover in when they blasted the stone, which was a highly dangerous job. One or two were killed when they were blasting the stone. They sheltered under wagons or flimsy sheds, which had been provided by the quarry owners, so my father was building stone and concrete shelters to make the job safer for the quarry men.

He used to look after the quarry houses and I would help him to repair the roofs for which he would pay me sixpence. The slates were always coming off. I would also help him to lay stone, which helped me quite a lot in learning to become a stonemason. I would also help him to build cow byres and pig sties, which were in big demand.

I had another job, which I did on a Sunday morning and evening. I used to pump the organ, a massive thing which stood at the back of the church where I puffed and blowed. It was not easy for a young boy so I used to take my friend along to help out. The organist was very forgetful about paying my weekly wage of sixpence. On one occasion four weeks passed by without payment. I said to myself "action must be taken to get my wages" so one Sunday morning when the congregation of about fifteen or so were in full voice I stopped pumping the organ and demanded my money from the organist. I got my four weeks' money plus a good telling off from the Rev. Jones, but he saw the funny side of it and blowers were hard to come by, so he put my wages up by 2d. I would also pump the organ during the week for funerals and weddings.

The highlight of our year was going to Redcar on the church outing. We were taken on two Scots Greys' coaches and we were all given sixpence to spend. We were provided with lunch and tea. We played on the beach all day if the weather was warm and if it was wet we were in the arcades all day. We would return home after a tiring day and look forward to the next year.

I did not know my Grandfather. He died before I was born. My Grandma lived at Aldbrough St. John. She was sister to Madeleine Carroll, the film star. One of the finest actresses of the 1930s and regarded as the epitome of English glamour and grace, Madeleine Carroll graced the screen and starred in Alfred Hitchcock's early suspense films, spy dramas, historical romances and other adventure stories. When I'd finished blowing the organ I would bike down to Grandma's and go for a walk with her then home for tea. Then go to Aldbrough Church on Sunday evening.

Quite a good boy! Grandma would give me a penny every Sunday. When we lived at Hutton Magna the whole family would walk to Aldbrough on a Sunday. Not every Sunday - it was the norm in those days - two or three times a year. It kept us out of mischief. My Grandma was just what a Grandma should be - kind and considerate. If anyone was ill she looked after him or her and laid them out when they died ready for burial. She was a saint. It was a sad day for me when she died and a great loss to the village of Aldbrough.

I served my apprenticeship as a stonemason with G. Shaw from Richmond. I would cycle there every day from Eppleby come rain, hail or snow, approximately 10 miles. I was laying stone nearly every day on new houses and flats and also doing repair work. I enjoyed my work as a stonemason, but did not like getting wet or riding the bike in the snow and ice in winter. Many times I had to carry the bike because of the snow. Those were the 'good old days', not as it is today with cars and such like. I had a motorbike once, a Royal Enfield, which eased the cycling a bit.

It was during this time that I was asked to help the local chimney sweep, who used to sweep quite a number of chimneys in his spare time. He used to travel on his bike after he finished work at the quarry. This is where I came into the picture. He charged 2s. 6d. per chimney. For some reason or other he was forever getting his brush stuck in the chimney either in the pot or the bend. He would then cycle to our house to see if I was at home so that I could help him to get his brush out. I had to climb on to the roof or go into the attic to cut out a brick to enable me to get hold of the rods and the brush. I used to charge him 5s. for this work. He got the brush stuck regularly so I don't know how he ever made any money at it. He would complain bitterly about me charging five bob, but there was nobody else to go to apart from me and father and, after all, I needed the money. He went to see the vicar to complain about my excessive charges and the vicar had a go at me about it.

I started work at 14 on a farm because I could not get an apprenticeship until later. It was during my cricket playing years that my brother and I had the opportunity to seek revenge on the Headmaster from my school days. We were playing the married men in a 'friendly'. I have to say that it wasn't very friendly!! When he came in to bat we bowled bodyliners and never hit the wicket. We had no intention of doing that, but to teach him a lesson that he would never forget. He threw his bat down a few times and appealed to the umpire, but to no avail. He eventually retired hurt!

I always remember working for Mr Manners of Forcett Valley. I really enjoyed it there. I looked after a Gales pony called Toby and would go to the station for coal every two weeks with the horse. I would drive the tractor and help the Horseman to muck out, also the herdsman and the shepherd. All were good men and it was a pleasure to work with them, but of course you always get the odd one out. This chap used to do all the repairs about the farm buildings, painting etc. One day the boss told him to paint the roof of the Dutch barn, which was oval and quite high, 30' approximately. He used a long brush attached to a long pole. Mr Manners said that I could help him by carrying one gallon of paint up to the top of the ladder and not to go any further. Tot would come and retrieve it. After one or two gallons, he wanted me to go up on to the roof of the Dutch barn and I refused. I told him the boss had said I must not go up past the top of the ladder. Tot lost his temper and threatened me with a thick ear and a kick up the backside. I still would not go on to the roof and he got really mad and started to come down off the roof to carry out his threat. I nipped down the ladder smartly, Tot following. When he got within a few feet of me I told him I would throw the paint at him. The lid was already off. He took no notice of my threat and advanced towards me. Then I threw the paint at him to save my skin. It covered him from top to toe. I ran off to where the shepherd was shearing the sheep. He saw what had happened and could not stop laughing. He said "stay here, I will look after you". After all, I was only 14. When the boss heard about it, he said I had done the right thing by not going on to the roof. He was not very pleased about losing a tin of paint and told Tot off for trying to make me go back onto the roof. I kept away from him for a day or two.

The next incident that I remember, I was in trouble with the same handyman: it was when we were riddling the potatoes and bagging them up into one cwt bags.

My job was to turn the handle of the riddle and also to pick off any green or bad potatoes and stones. Tot was bagging them up and if one got past it was his job to stop the riddle and throw it off into the rubbish. This particular day it was my turn to pick off the bad ones. The herdsman who looked after the cows was shovelling in the potatoes when a big juicy one came past me and I let it go. When Tot saw it he told Mary who was turning the handle to stop and said "Boy, you have let one come past you". I said I had not seen it. He picked it up and threw it at me. I ducked and it hit the chap who was shovelling the potatoes. He had not forgotten the paint!

I had a word with the herdsman who it had hit and said "next time we will sort him out". It was not long before another juicy one came along, but I retrieved this one. I had it in my hand and said "Look Tot what I have got" and I let fly with the rotten potato and hit him in the face with it. There was all hell let loose. We were in a barn with the door shut. I ran around the potato machine with Tot after me, getting wilder by the minute. I was shouting to Mary to open the door so I could get out. I wanted to get out of that place otherwise he would have killed me. Mary did get the door open; I escaped and didn't go back that day. Once again I was sent for by Mr Manners to explain what I had done to Tot. He could not help but smile when he heard from the others what had taken place. Tot and I did become good friends later when I helped him out on numerous occasions, but he was a character in more ways than one.

Work was still going on, milking the cows, 13 a day, laying stone etc. On an evening we played billiards and joined the Reading Room at Forcett where they had a table, on which we played regularly. As a lad my father used to look after the table. He would brush and iron it nearly every night. During this time the nurses who used to look after the babies were billeted at the Big Hall. Sometimes there were about twelve to fifteen nurses staying there towards the end of the war. There was a post box built into the wall of the Reading Room. This box had a flap on it, which made a noise when anyone posted a letter. That was the signal for my mate and I to dash outside and meet the nurses. There were always two. It was months before some of the club members tumbled to the fact that we were going out with these different girls every night, especially during the winter months. We were only about 16 or 17 years old.

The Women's Institute was very active in all the villages. Dancing and playing whist and darts was usual in those days and there was always a prize to be won. It was at one of the dances at Ovington I had a chat to the Catholic Priest about turning out the children during prayers because we weren't Catholic. I asked how he could do it as it says in the Bible "suffer the little children to come unto me". He did not give me a satisfactory answer. This would not happen today, but you can take it from me it happened then. I was not very pleased.

By this time I had lost my sister Kathleen when she was 13. What a loss that was. She was the apple of my mother and father's eye. She had appendicitis and they could not get her to the hospital on time. The fact that we had a lot of brothers and sisters did not lessen the pain, it was still a dreadful shock.

We had earth closets in those days and chamber pots were used. Thank the Lord for proper toilets and drainage. It was not very hygienic and some houses - especially farmhouses - had two or three biddies with three seats where you sat side by side. I know of one still in existence today, not in use, but used as a store. It was only in the 1960s that we all got modernised with running water and flush toilets for the poor. The rich had them when they first came out.

I used to milk 13 cows on a morning and again at night. I lived in with the farmer and his wife and a lad called John who also milked 13 cows, the same as me. I never went short of milk and used to get a pint mug every night when I went to bed. It was coming up to Christmas and the farmer's wife had her mother to stay over Christmas. She was a bit of a lass who liked to play tricks on you. I went upstairs one night and she had filled my side of the bed with holly. I wondered what the lumps were in the bed. The candlelight was not very good and John and I had to sleep in the same double bed with just our long shirts on. We couldn't afford pyjamas. When I saw this and what they had done I was furious. I moved all the holly onto John's side and then went downstairs to read a book in the kitchen.

I never said a word to John. He had been out to see his Aunt and Uncle who lived just a mile or two down the road at Ravensworth. We had our suppers then went upstairs to bed. We got changed and were just going to get into bed when I blew the candle out, which wasn't very nice of me. John landed on the holly and cried out. By this time the farmer's wife and her mother had crept upstairs to listen through the door, when they heard John shout about the holly prickling his bottom. He took some calming down. When I lit the candle and he saw the holly, he went mad and it was quite a job to control him. He said "how could you play such a rotten trick on me!" When I explained it was the farmer's wife and her mother and said we must get our own back, John was not very keen because he was the blue eyed boy.

I told him I was going to place the holly in the mother's bed because they had not come to bed yet. John thought that was a good idea, since his bottom was still stinging. Off we set along the landing with the holly in our hands, nobody in sight. We had got into the spare bedroom where she was staying, pulled the sheets back and placed the holly so she would land on it the same as she had done to me and John. As we were closing the door, they caught us. They had canes in their hands; consequently we got a caning. Poor John! His bottom was really sore and even worse after the caning.

When I worked at Catterick, helping to build the NAFFI Club for nearly two years, I used to catch a rabbit or two and raffle them once a week. I didn't have any trouble selling tickets at sixpence each. Food was not easy to get even then. I made more out of the raffle than I did working.

My father worked for the same firm as me along with some other masons. I used to collect up all the blunt tools every week and take them with the wagon driver to the blacksmith to get them sharpened. The stone that was being dressed on the site was limestone from a local quarry and was very hard. The tools, chisels, bolsters, etc, were all marked with the Mason mark. They all had one, including me. We had a banker hand who was called Mark. He dressed stone only and did not lay any. That is why he was called a banker hand. He had to get the stone ready for the masons to lay it. We all dressed the stone as he could not keep four masons going on his own. Mark was a Methodist and did not gamble as it was against his religion. I tried for weeks to sell him a raffle ticket, but to no avail. Food was still rationed and meat was expensive. Then one day he relented and bought a ticket. He did not win, but he never heard the last of it when word got around the site that Mark had bought a ticket.

A lot of hard work was done on that site, by hand digging 6ft down for drains and mixing and wheeling the concrete by barrows. It was a hard life - 8am till 5 o'clock at night. We were dropped off by the works bus at Manfield Road Ends, then we biked home from there.

My first car was an experience. The local Director of the Quarry wanted a garage building with a loo and a window overlooking the beck so he could see what was going on.   He was also Superintendent of the Specials at Middlesbrough.   He wanted me to build his garage in stone and he would give me the car and trailer for building the garage. The car was a blue Jowitt and in good condition. When I saw the car I had no hesitation in agreeing to build the garage and loo. The joiner from the quarry would do the joinery work. That is how I got my first car. All the lads in the village envied me.   One lad called Ken used to come and clean and polish it just to get a ride to our house and back, which was about quarter of a mile. We went to cricket and dances etc. I was never short of friends who always wanted a lift. The village bobby played cricket and used to ride in it, too. One day he said to me "Bill, don't you think you should get that car taxed. It is long overdue". I had never given it a thought that I needed to pay tax. The tax had long since run out.   What a decent bobby he was, he kept law and order in our village. We didn't have the burglars and vandalism that we have today. They definitely were the 'good old days' even though there was not much money.

I continued to play football and cricket for a number of years to come, which I enjoyed immensely. I played in goal and was many times pushed through the goal for holding on to the ball. You could do that in those days, it was tough. The leather ball took some kicking when it was wet, not like it is today, what I have seen of them. When my brother was playing he had to go for trials at Newcastle and I went with him to keep an eye on him. I was courting a girl who worked at the big hall at Forcett and she lived at Wallsend with her mother so we stayed with them. We stayed at Wallsend and travelled in to Newcastle. I also played at Newcastle, in goal. They signed my brother, but not me. I had the job of getting the expenses off the manager, Mr Martin, the manager between 1948-50, who tried to diddle me out of them. I told him I would go to the newspapers. He soon paid up! He did not want any bad publicity, which was what I was counting on.

As lads we still went out rabbiting. In those days I had a catapult which I regularly used to kill a rabbit for food for the family. One night my mate and I heard that a cock pheasant had landed in a holly tree at the bottom of the garden of a retired farmer and it was sleeping there every night. He was looking after it for Christmas, when he thought it would be his. So one night we visited his back garden with a torch and a catapult and bagged the pheasant. The problem was who was going to have the bird, so we tossed up and I won. It did not go far between a large family, but it was a luxury. The same applied to the rabbits and we did after all have to be fed. Life was hard and if my father was on the dole, and one of my sisters got a job, he lost money because she was working. If that happened today they would all be on strike.

One night we all went out with the long net. We thought this lad had the rabbit rights (in other words, permission). It was only when we had caught 30 or more that he said he was poaching and we all scarpered! I remember poachers caught one lad in our village when he was courting and was held by them for two hours until they had got all the rabbits out of the sets. He was in real trouble when he got home and he never went that way again. It must have been one hell of an experience being held captive for that amount of time. Especially when he had only been courting a girl.

I remember one day Lily, my second elder sister, and her husband Albert came to stay for the night. The room we were sleeping in had three beds, so my brothers and I had to double-up to let Albert have a bed for the night. Albert kept saying,

"Are you asleep yet?" But we spent most of the night wide-awake - much to the annoyance of Albert. Happy Days!

CHAPTER TWO

I left Shaw's and came to work in Darlington for a local builder, J. W. Richardson. I bought a motorcycle, a Royal Enfield. It was the only motorcycle I knew that went backwards. I always had to start it twice, but it still got me there and back. I had to go for a test and came down to Darlington to take it. The examiner who took the test did not pass many people, I think she had a chip on her shoulder. I remember the day it was my test for the motorbike. I was feeling a bit emotional about taking it, especially when I heard that the pass rate was less than 10 out of 100.

You can imagine the strain of meeting this woman. I had an appointment on the morning at 11 am, I was on time and so was the test examiner. She asked me a few questions, which I answered correctly, then she told me to start up my motorbike and go round the block. This was Grange Road and Coniscliffe Road in a square. She said she would step off the pavement, at which point I should make an emergency stop. I said to her "I would not do that if I were you, you could get killed if my brakes don't pull me up". The look she gave me! I knew I would not pass after saying this and I did not. I was one of the 90% failures. They did remove her after various complaints. Things got back to normal then.

We once had to fit a new ceiling in a house in Albert Road near Bank Top off Neasham Road, where the houses were in little streets and my father used to do a lot of work for a landlord who owned quite a number of these houses. Part of the ceiling had come down in the bedroom and it was urgent. My father asked me if I would do it after I finished work on the Friday, so I said Tony and I would do it on the Saturday as it would take us all day, but I would get it done. So we loaded the trailer up with battens and a few drums to stand on, plasterboard and plaster etc. When we got there the bed and wardrobe were still in the room. So we moved what we could out of the room, but left the bed which we covered up with sheets and then we knocked down the rest of the ceiling which was in a terrible state and the dust and the muck was all over the house.

Left: Family ties. My
grandmother at the family home
in Aldbrough St. John in the late
1800s - the house is still there
Below: At play. Me (second left)
with my brothers and sisters at
Whorlton Lido

The woman of the house was playing war because the dust had gone downstairs and was everywhere. By dinnertime the ceiling was boarded and ready for plastering. We had our lunch outside in the car and I started to get ready for plastering. The woman came into the bedroom and asked me how long we were going to be and I said we should get finished by 4 o'clock. She said to me "You should have been finished by 12 o'clock" and I said "Not a hope!" She then said she wanted to use the bedroom as quick as possible and I said I would do my best. Tony in the meantime was downstairs getting water to mix the plaster.

When he came back he said the kitchen was full of men - five or six of them sitting about. The men said "How long will you be?" Tony said "We have just got started with the plastering". I thought this is rather strange - the woman hurrying me and wanting the bedroom, there's something queer going on here. So I went downstairs and sure enough Tony was right, there were men in the kitchen and I thought, like Tony, that they had come up for a game of cards. While we were plastering there were noises from the other bedrooms. There were only three bedrooms and we were working in the front bedroom. I said to Tony "I think we are in a house of disrepute - in other words a brothel!" He said "Never! The quicker we get out of here, the better!"

Tony and I were only a couple of country lads and did not know very much about this sort of thing going on in houses. The woman came upstairs and asked me again how long we were going to be, so I said to her "Why are you in such a hurry to get us out? Are you on nightshift?" She looked at me and said, "You are losing me money! If you don't know what's going on then I'm not telling you. The quicker you get that bloody ceiling done, the better it is for me".

I was amazed that such a thing was happening so close to us. I said to Tony "I was right, it is a brothel and the quicker we get finished here the better" and that is what we did. When I got home and told my father about it, he said the experience would do us both the world of good and it certainly did. It was an experience that Tony and I never forgot and never shall.

I bought two old cottages for £35.50 to start up as a builder. The deal was done in the Travellers Rest at Eppleby and my pal Stan witnessed the deal and I paid over the cash. I then had to go to a solicitor for the Stamp Duty and I got a telling off for not going to them in the first place. I had done them out of money by buying it like that. I altered it a little bit and used part as a garage for the Jowitt which was still being run regularly, and I filled the rest up with hens and material. I kept the hens for a year or two then got rid of them, as I did not have the time to look after them.

I was still working for firms building houses. One day I asked the Manager for a 1d pay rise and he refused. I would be getting more than him, but I told him I was a craftsman. I had been working on a stone job in the country and I was getting uneasy about working for someone else. I wanted to start up on my own. This was a golden opportunity to make a break and begin work on my own, which I did. The architect who worked on the site was very upset when he heard I was leaving, because I was the only stonemason there and they were hard to come by then.

Later the architect told me he had a village hall to build and would I give him a quote for it. When he told me it was in my own village, I immediately said yes and especially when he told me who else was going to quote, the same firm who would not give me a 1d rise. I was overjoyed. That was the golden opportunity for which I had been waiting. I got the job and was £2,500 below them. At this particular time I was courting a farmer's daughter, a solicitor's clerk and a tax inspector. My car was very busy and I remember during the month of December a few days before Christmas, coming back from dropping off one of the three, I was pulled up by a policeman on Winston Bridge who asked me if I had any birds in the back, and when I told him I had one in the back he was not amused and made me get out of the car and open the boot. To his surprise there was nothing there. People at that time were poaching chickens and turkeys. Times were so bad then that I still continued catching a rabbit or so.

We had no phone in our house and these girls would ring the garage owner up. I had given them his number and he used to complain about the number of calls he received from the girls. I had been courting Laura seriously for some time: we got married and we have been married to this day. It was after I got married that I started up on my own as a builder. The village hall was my first job. What a challenge that was, especially when I had to employ labour. I was fortunate to have my brother who was serving his national service. He was in the Medical Corps and used to inject the soldiers on the morning then come to work for me for an hour when he could. The reason he was at Catterick was because my father was very ill and he got compassionate leave. We had 12 weeks to build the hall and I built it in six weeks. They could not pay me and that nearly broke me.

After the village hall I got the contract for building stone shelters for the Rural District in Darlington for £98 which I completed at the rate of one a week with the help of my brother-in-law, Albert. After building three I found out that the Rural District Council was paying £110 for brick shelters, so I went on strike. After a lot of arguments and a couple of meetings, I got an extra £12. The shelters are still standing to this day.

I built one of these shelters in a village, near the church, along with many others for the Rural District of Darlington. There was a village shop near to where we were building this particular shelter and the lady owner of the shop was very helpful to us and allowed me to use their water and to store our tools and barrows etc at the back of the premises. It was during the construction of this shelter, while we were putting in the foundations, that the trenches were open, so in order to make it safe to the public we covered it over and placed three red lights around it before finishing for the day.

Next morning, Albert my brother-in-law said that one of the red lights was missing. This was at 8 o'clock in the morning! After a bit of searching we eventually found it - nailed to the shop door - still lit and with a note on it saying "I knocked on the door, but did not get an answer"!

The shopkeeper was not at all amused, but we apologised to her and we never used the red lights on the stone shelters again. Although I still have them in my office to this day.

During this time I lost my daughter and that tragedy has been with me over the years and also with my wife Laura. But life has to go on and I continued to build

With all Good Wishes

Above left: Happy times. Me as a young boy

Above right: Workmates. My father with Tommy Richmond in the 1950s

Centre bottom: Hard graft. My father (centre) with labourers

houses, village halls, factories, etc. and repairs which I rather liked and I met a lot of nice people as well as bad! I recall the stone house I built at a village in the country. It was solid stone - 12" on the bed and solid brick externally. Everything went wrong. The owner was away in Ireland on holiday and the architects were left in charge. I had 27 variation orders, which were not worth the paper they were written on. When the owner returned from holiday, the tiles had been altered, Hardrow slates instead of Westmoreland slates, doors were wrong. One thing he did not find wrong was the stonework, so he wanted an arbitration. My solicitor agreed to this and I spent three days in the witness box at a local hotel in the town. I lost the case, costing me nearly £10,000, which was one of the biggest shocks of my life.

I had built the stone bungalow for nothing. I had to pay the money back every month, which was crippling. I wanted to go bankrupt, but Laura said it would be a stain on my character, so I paid up monthly. They were very hard times indeed because I was paying for my son Graeme to go to private school. I learned a hard lesson in life about the people I dealt with at that particular time, but they say if you live long enough you will see your day with them and I did. The architect got a divorce and broke his legs in a fall. The other architect also had things happen to him. The owner of the bungalow also fell on bad times and his wife became unwell. It just shows what happens, justice was seen to be done, but I was still paying for their mistakes.

I continued to pay what the arbitrator said just to keep my good name, it was very hard, but I had some good friends who helped me out. After all I still had a mortgage on my house and I was also sending my son to a private school. They looked after me and gave me work. One in particular was very kind to me. He went out of his way to get me work and I will be forever grateful to him. He was a Managing Director of a large firm in Darlington and a well-known local figure.

CHAPTER THREE

It was around about the sixties that I was asked by the Police if I would go out on emergency work, because the builder who did it was retiring and I said I would, because I was still paying back money from the arbitration. Sergeant Ord was the man who set me on the road re boarding up. I was to owe my thanks to him for the following 35 years.

I will let you into the secrets of boarding up in the middle of the night. Word got around that I was able to go anywhere and board up. In the beginning it was quite easy. People would occasionally walk through glass doors or even large windows. One lady even parked her car in the jeweller's shop. She said she didn't see the bend in the road. The shop in question was in Grange Road. She was driving down Coniscliffe Road. We had to push the car out before we could get her out.

It was the practice of the police 35 years ago or so to ring me and tell me where to go, but in the middle of the night I sometimes could not hear the phone ringing. The Sergeant on duty would send a Constable up to my house on his bike and he would throw stones at my bedroom window to waken me up. He would then pedal back downtown. I would get out the pick up with the boards on and off I would go - often beating him to the place where the windows were to be boarded up. I was the only one doing this service during the middle of the night and as the years went by I got quite used to it. Some nights I was never in and had to call out one of my men if there were a lot of windows broken. I was going from one job to another and I needed the help.

Before I start writing about the things that happened to me during the last 35 years, which are quite true, I must tell you that my building business continued to grow and flourish. I rented a yard in King William Street. That was an experience! It belonged to the Railway where they used to keep the horses etc during the late 1800s early 1900s. I stayed there for some years and during the time I was in occupation it rained in and brought down part of the ceiling up in the joiner's shop. In the early days this had been the hayloft for the coach horses. There we found a very old lamp, which I still have stored away to this day.

In 1963 I joined the Lingfield Ward Committee and played an active part in that Committee i.e. going to the meetings, raising money, coffee mornings canvassing, etc. By far the most popular event was the Jumble Sale. This was the highlight of the calendar for the people in the Ward who would arrive in droves to try and get the bargains, which they usually did. Some of the men (including myself) would model some of the clothes, hats etc. so that we could get more money. It was always a good night and we raised quite a bit of money. Sadly these days everything goes to the charity shops and jumble sales have become a thing of the past, so we have to look elsewhere for our funds.

In those days ward Council elections were held every year. There was one Councillor up for election in each ward in the town and this particular year it was Lingfield's turn to have the election for one Councillor. We had a meeting of the ward committee and they suggested that I stand as the next Conservative candidate for Lingfield. I agreed, very reluctantly because I was building and my business was quite busy and I did not think I had time to stand. Then came the tricky part. I had to get Laura's agreement. After all I did not know what pitfalls I was letting myself in for.

Laura agreed that I should put my name forward as the Conservative candidate in the Ward. I then rang the chairman of the Ward to tell him that I would stand. After a few days I had a telephone call from the Agent of the Association who asked me if he and the Chairman of the Association could come to see me. I agreed that they could come and see me one evening at about 7 o'clock. They stayed for approximately 1½ hours grilling me to see that I was a suitable person to stand i.e. my character, criminal record, etc. If I had known of the questions I was going to be asked I don't think I would have stood for the Council, but that was what they did in those days. They wanted to be sure that I was a proper person to represent the people.

After they left I said to Laura "I'm not bothered if I don't stand after the grilling I've had!"

It is not like that today, you have a job to get people to stand and they don't get grilled like that.

Lingfield was not a safe seat: it was held by the independents and Labour and had not been held by the Conservatives for a long time. The chap whose seat I was trying to gain was the deputy Mayor and was to become Mayor of Darlington in the May. I had not one chance of winning according to the opposition. It never worried me. I worked hard knocking on doors. I practically knocked on every door in the ward myself. That is where the fun started.

After I had been canvassing for a week I went for a drink in the local pub, a big haunt for the Labour councillors and the Aldermen. In those days that is where they used to meet to discuss policies. I was with two of my friends having a pint which we did once or twice a week in the same pub. I was talking to the landlord about the election when a hand tapped me on the shoulder and this man said "I know why you and the other builder (who, incidentally, was standing in another ward) are standing to get on the council. To get all the building contracts and gain ..."

He had no sooner said "gain" when I picked him up by the lapels of his jacket and threw him to one side of the room. He fell on the table where all the Councillors and Aldermen were sitting. The lounge fell totally silent and the Labour Councillor whom I had thrown across the room left the pub. Alderman Buckberry said "he has been asking for that for some time, but the sad thing about it is that he did not knock any pints off the table. If he had only spread his legs we would have got our glasses filled, because they were nearly empty!"

A call was made to the The Northern Echo and the Evening Despatch newspapers. I also received a solicitors letter and you can imagine what Laura said about the write up in the paper two days later.

She said I must tell them I was not standing for the Council, but I was determined to stand to prove to him that I was standing because of the people in the ward. The publicity was fair and the Labour council could not do anything about it because it happened after 10 o'clock: the saga kept going right up to two days before the election.

Much to my surprise I won the seat for six years until 1971 when I was defeated and it was another two years before I was elected again in the West End and I have served the people of the west end for the last 31 years.

I stayed at King William Street for a few years and built a lot of houses etc from there and boarded up a lot of windows and doors. A local undertaker approached me about buying the whole of his Estate, which included seven houses, and 10 garages and the joiners' shops included the mortuary. We met to discuss the price and he started putting conditions on. One was that I would look after his hens and cockerel and provide him with a dozen eggs a week as long as they were laying. He was on to a good thing. I reluctantly agreed, but before I agreed to the sale of the land, houses and garages and his workshops, I said that I had a condition that I would like to be included in the contract. That the rents of the houses would go up by 50% and that he would have to collect them. He hummed and harred a bit, after all he had known all of the tenants for years, they were his friends and I was just a newcomer. That is when the fun began when I moved into the premises. The tenants wanted me to do all sorts of work. It was a battle of wits. I did some things, but not all. They were quite nice people.

However, the thing that worried me the most was feeding those hens, and especially the cockerel. The first day that I fed them I went into the pen because they had a long pen to run in and as I walked out of the door the cockerel got me by the neck. Will only lived next door and when I told him about this, he said I should have walked out backwards, he won't bother you then. I was so mad I threatened to sell the lot of them, but I kept them anyway. When we started a new apprentice either bricklayer or joiner, his first job was to feed the hens. We would be standing in the joiners' shop on the first floor when he went in. That was the time the cockerel initiated him and this went on for as long as those hens were there. I replaced the hens twice, but still kept the cockerel.

The other thing I did not like was going there in the middle of the night to pick up the boards, which were stored in the mortuary. On the shelves were shoeboxes filled with ashes. When relatives would not have them, Will stored them there. This was the first time we had seen them because we could not see them from the ground. I approached Will about them and asked him what we were going to do about them. He said put them in a barrow and I will get rid of them. What he did with them I don't know, but he had the biggest apples and roses in the town. There wasn't a lot he could do; he was a very old man. I would say that they found their resting place.

I was building two semi-detached houses in town and as there were only two I quickly sold them. An old lady came along with a carrier bag with £3,500 in notes and wanted to buy one of the semis. I told her they were already sold and I could not do anything, but I told her my house was up for sale and she said "I will have a look at it". She fell in love with it and wanted me to take the money, but I did not. I informed my solicitor who would not believe it, but the deal went through and she paid the money to the solicitors.

I also remember building a very large extension in stone in the country. When we came to settle the bill, he knocked £40 off and would not pay. He said it would go towards the cost of tea and biscuits, which he provided us with during the time we were building it. This was a load of cobblers. We brought our own flasks and sandwiches. It was my profit. I took the case to my solicitors and he thought I was pulling his leg. Especially the bit about tea and biscuits! He was reluctant to pay, but he did pay up eventually.

The houses in Eastbourne Road were in need of a lot of money spending on them and I could not afford to do this as the rents were so low. People were living in these houses for 7s. 6d., 3s. 6d. and 2s. 6d. per week. Consequently the Council condemned the houses. We then submitted plans for the whole site to be built on, which I did and subsequently named it Kay Grove after my mother. There is a story about the name, but that was political. I was a member of the Borough Council.

CHAPTER FOUR

I was still boarding up - Darlington, Newton Aycliffe, Bishop Auckland, Crook, Hartlepool, Middlesbrough, Stockton, Thornaby, Redcar, Northallerton and Richmond. The call would come in from the police or others i.e. private houses and a lot of shops who also had my number, and of course who would answer the phone first, but Laura. By this time we had the phone installed in the bedroom. If it was before 11 o'clock, Laura would ring me. The pick-up being loaded at all times, I was ready to go hail rain or snow.

A particular experience I had was at the Salvation Army Hostel (now pulled down) on the edge of the new ring road. The Major who was in charge there asked me if I could meet him after 5pm to discuss alterations to the hostel regarding Fire Regulations. At the time I was building houses and was wearing a pair of wellies. When I went to see him I did not have time to change and so consequently went there straight from work. I washed my wellies on site then went to see the Major. Whilst I was waiting to see the Major all the down-and-outs were booking in for a bed for the night. They also got an evening meal, which smelt very nice. I was sitting by myself, minding my own business, when one of the tough-looking types looked down at my wellies, which were practically new, and said "They are nice wellies, you won't have them by morning!" I looked him straight in the eye and said, "I have got news for you, I'm not staying the night!" He looked most surprised. He had thought I was a down-and-out and was looking for a place to kip for the night. I mentioned it to the Major, who though it was very funny and asked if he could use it in his sermon on Sunday. The theme being that you could not judge a man by the clothes he wore. As a churchman myself I said "yes". When Laura heard about it she was not very pleased. I told her I had no fleas on me. When a new customer arrives at the hostel they put him straight in the bath and delouse him so I was very lucky to escape!

After I had measured up, I had to go to the top floor where a really old gentleman was in bed ill. The Major told me that all he wanted to do was lie in bed. I said "Well, we will have to get him out of that bed because the room has to be altered! We don't want to be held up." I went over to the bed and said that I was the undertaker and that I had heard he was not very well and had popped in to measure him up. I had my 3ft. rule. He opened his eyes and said that he was feeling much better. Next day he was up for his breakfast. The Major was amazed what could be done with a bit of diplomacy. This enabled me to finish the contract on time for Christmas and the man went back to work. All's well that ends well!

We continued to board up the shops in the town etc. on a very large scale. I remember one night being called out to Hartlepool. I had got a new Ford pick-up. When I was travelling to Hartlepool, I was trying to get there as quickly as possible and was pulled up by the traffic police. They wanted to know where I was going. It was well past 1am and they asked me for the vehicle's registration number and wanted to know where I'd stolen the 8' x 4' boards I was carrying. I could not remember the number as I'd only had the pick-up for a few days.

The officer then proceeded to get out his book and was going to charge me, when I told him that the Sergeant had sent for me to board up three windows in the town centre and that was the reason for me speeding, to get there as fast as I could. The officer said "Why didn't you tell me this in the first place". I said "You did not ask. You thought I had stolen the pick-up". They then escorted me to the broken windows, which I boarded up. Then I went back home to my bed. Sleep! I did not get a lot of that in those days. I was out three or four times a night. Sometimes my joiners would not answer the phone. I remember Tom, who used to work for me, did not have the phone in. I used to go and knock him up and take him with me. One New Year's Eve after 12.30 we went to Ken Warne's shop in Cleveland Avenue to board up a large window at the shop. After we had finished Ken brought out a third of a bottle of Long John Scotch. Tom being a Scotsman relished this and we sat outside and first footed the New Year in. Tom was quite merry when I dropped him off.

Around the same time we were doing some work for St. John's Church in Yarm

Road. We were working on the tower and the roof when we were asked to take down the flagpole because it was rotten and erect a new pole, which had to be painted white. The pole was over 20 ft. high and there was very little parapet around the tower, making it very difficult to fit. By the time we got all the fittings on and got it assembled, the paintwork was looking shabby. The vicar asked me if it was possible to paint it. Tom heard him say this and said he would do it. He said he would shin up the pole and paint it as he came down. The paint tin was strapped to his head by string and the brush he held in his teeth. The ladder we had on the roof was very short - approximately 6ft. He said he used to shin up and down a pole like this when he was in the Navy. The vicar and I were very grateful to him.

The next incident which happened to me was on a very frosty night not far from where I lived. A garage window went through late at night. It was so cold that I had gloves on while I was boarding up. I nailed my glove to the board. The policeman thought I was drunk. I know I had been down the club that night, but I said to him "I always do that when I want to take off my glove, especially when I have to straighten the nails, before driving them home. Then I don't lose it!" Whether he believed me or not is a matter of opinion. He thought I was drunk talking about bent nails. It was my job or the apprentice's job to straighten the nails. It was worth the effort and saved me money. Everybody complained about the bent nails, but they did the job. After all you took them out of the board the next day and straightened them and used them again. I did occasionally buy new ones, but only when we were getting a bit low. The same applied to the boards. I used the same ones over and over again.

CHAPTER FIVE

I had been approached to join the Council in 1965. What a year that was! I had been nominated as the candidate for the May election, along with a number of distinguished people: estate agents, builders, auctioneers, solicitors, hairdressers, etc. Another builder and I were accused of going on the Town Council for gain. I could write another book about my 35 years on the Council - The ups and downs of a local Councillor - which I am sure would make very interesting reading.

Things were getting better regarding work etc. I was still boarding up. One night in Skinnergate, a very large window was broken by vandals. The window in question was 12' x 9' and there were four or more of these in Bainbridge Barkers. There was a gale blowing that night and it was getting worse. When I got there, there were large pieces of glass ready to fall out on to the pavement. I always carried long pieces of 2" x 2" on the pickup to knock out any damaged glass. I got the 2" x 2" and was just going to knock out the last piece when the wind caught me and sent me through the next window and broke it. I was lucky I was not hurt. The porter heard the crash and asked me if I'd seen the vandals. I dare not say that it was me who had broken it. I told a white lie and said "they were like lightening! Broke it and ran like hell on to the High Row!" I then had to make that window safe as well.

I remember boarding up the door of a well known tailor in Northgate. It was an aluminum door and I used two pieces of board - one on either side then hammered a 5" or 6" nail through and bent it over. To do this securely I needed someone at the other side to hold the plywood. The only person who was around at the time was the manager. I knocked the nail through when he was holding up the board with his hand. The nail went straight through his hand close to his fingers. He let out a scream "you have nailed my hand to the board" he shouted. I immediately rushed round to the back of the door and saw the nail through his hand. I said I was very sorry, he must have had his hand in the wrong place. While he wasn't looking I hit the nail and drove it back through the board. He said he would have to go to the hospital for treatment. I said he would have to wait until we had finished boarding up, so he sent for his wife, who was not very pleased, and she took him to the hospital.

A week or two later the high winds blew out three windows and I had to board them up at around 9.30 p.m. The wind was blowing at gale force and the manager helped me take off the 8' x 4' boards. As we were on the main road there were railings around the pavement to prevent people from walking on the road. We had just got hold of a board when the wind came in such force that it lifted him and me over the railings and into the middle of the road where a double-decker bus was coming. The driver got very irate and asked what the hell we were playing at. I did not bother to explain to him, but got the board back and started to board up. After we boarded up the three windows, the manager told me that the shop was going to be altered and that the work would not take place for a few weeks. So I told him that I would put the boards on hire at £1 per day, per board. Twelve boards were used. The shop did not get altered until nearly a year later and they continued to pay by cheque every month until the last two or three months. Then they wrote me a letter asking me to call and see the Manager to discuss the hire arrangements. He suggested that I get two suits instead of the money for a month. You can imagine my surprise at this offer. I told him in no uncertain terms that I bought my suits from a private tailor. He wasn't very pleased about that. I said I would just take the money, so they continued to pay. I did not charge them for the bent nails as an extra!

I remember going to another job on Albert Hill on the estate where people used to rent buildings and offices. I could not find the place. What I did find were two Alsations running loose. I got out of the pick-up to try and find the premises to board up, when about 50 yards away these two dogs were heading straight for me. I turned and ran back to the pick-up and just made it by the skin of my teeth. No sooner had I closed the door, when these two dogs slammed into the side of the door, growling and barking. I was lucky that night, the police rescued me and took me to the broken windows and sorted out the dog owners. I could have been killed.

On another night I was boarding up a shop in Yarm Road when a woman came

Top: Learning me trade. Me (middle) with a couple of masons from whom I learned my craft, Mark Haslop (left) and Tommy Richmond
Bottom: Film star. Madeleine Carroll, the most famous, and glamorous, member of our family!

running down Yarm Road with nothing on but a slip. I felt very embarrassed. So did the shopkeeper when I invited her into the shop and he gave me a good ticking off. He said his wife would not like to see a half-clad lady in his shop, but I only did it because I could see that the lady in question was distressed. She only wanted to go shopping, so I told her this shop had just opened so that we could get her in and ring the police to take her away. She had run away from a home further up town. It was a case of helping the poor lady. I would do the same thing again if I had to.

On another occasion I was making one hell of a noise in the middle of the night while boarding up and sawing. This man came charging out of his house and threatening me and saying he would knock my 'bloody head' off if I didn't stop banging and why did I not use a rubber hammer as I had woken all the kids up and his wife. The police were in attendance at the time. He got abusive especially when I said "You are bloody barmy!" The policeman told him we could not board up without making a noise, that included knocking nails into boards.

I was called out at 3am to board up a large window in a shop at Bolton, Lancashire. I told him I would go if they could not get anybody else and he said he could not get anybody else as he had tried and as I was only thirty minutes away would I get there as soon as I could because the shopkeeper was waiting. When I told him it was near Blackpool he said he knew that and I said I lived in Darlington, approximately 100 miles away. If you insist I will go, I told him, but it will cost you a lot of money. He said he wasn't worried about the money. I said I would take my wife and my son and we would spend the rest of the day in Blackpool, but it will take me a few hours to get there. I think I may have made a great mistake. Can I ring you back? I said "of course!", but I'm still waiting for the call. What a mistake! I have had a few calls like that one. My fame as the fastest board up man in the land must have spread!

Another incident occurred at Cockerton at Lloyds Bank when I boarded up the shop after a burglary. That was quite a break-in! They did not get anything, but certainly caused some damage. When we were finished boarding up the Manager gave me one of their black horse money boxes and the policeman got one too. I told him it was bad luck if he did not put some money in for luck. We did not get any, he was quite mean I thought. I gave my money box to my son Graeme and I did put a shilling in to start him off saving.

We were still building village halls and working on the farms. I once stayed all night at a farm in North Yorkshire just to get the final payment of £2,000, which the farmer owed me. He wouldn't pay me the final payment so I said "I'm staying until you pay". I had my supper with them and he kept saying "isn't it time you were going home?" I kept on saying I would go when he gave me the cheque. They were good Methodists and did not drink. All I was having was tea, but the supper was good. I slept on the settee till next morning and had breakfast with them. By this time I was becoming an embarrassment to him as his farm hands were coming in to take their orders. I knew most of them and they thought I was after the farmer's wife, but it was the £2,000 I was after, not her. The farmer got so sick of me hanging around that he decided to pay up, but I had to promise not to bank the cheque straight away because it might bounce. I travelled back home as quickly as I could. Laura kept asking me if I had got the money. I said yes, but that I could not put it in the bank. I honoured his wish and the cheque cleared. I think he sold some of his cows.

Whilst on the subject of farmers, I worked for quite a few in the early days and in particular, two brothers who lived a mile or so away from each other. I would go to Tom's farm and he would say "I can't pay you yet, not till the end of the month". I used to say that I had my men to pay and I could not wait till the end of the month. I said that if he did not pay then I would not be going to see his brother Joe who always wanted work doing while I was at Tom's. I said I would have to ring Joe up and cancel the work. He said "Don't do that! I will pay you now so that Joe does not hear about it!"

I remember Tony, one of my lads, was repairing the old Pantiles above the stable when the whole of the roof caved in and Tony fell through the roof, through the ceiling and into the loose box where his best horse was. He landed in the hay rack, which fitted into the corner of the stable and landed with his two legs sticking out of the hay rack. The horse went mad. It took some time to get him out of there. I had to send for one of the farm hands and after a struggle we managed to get him out by tying a rope around his middle and pulling him out without damage to himself, but plenty of damage to the ceiling and stable roof. It was a plastered ceiling. They looked after their horses in those days!

The farm hands who lived in the farmhouse ate by themselves in the kitchen with the maids and cook but not until after the farmer and his wife and family had eaten. Even then they didn't get the same as the family, but had to make do with the scraps that were left. I was very lucky when I stayed on the farms as a lad. I lived with the family. I only stayed a few months with one farmer who was a gentleman farmer and did not work. I had to stay in their large bedroom with two other farm workers. We had to use the chamber pot and when it got full we would empty it out of the window on to the laurel bush or the lawn. Tot used to say to me during the summer "I don't know what is the matter with that laurel bush and the lawn!" I didn't dare tell him that it was the contents of the chamber pot that was doing all the damage. After all, Joe used to get a few pints of beer and could not use the upstairs loo. I did see life even though I was only 14.

Joe was a home man and loved his horses, which after all did all the ploughing, harrowing, rolling and cutting grass all day. They had a Fordson tractor, but the work was done mostly by the Clydesdales. Boy were they big! Especially to me when I used to try to get the braffins over their heads.

On threshing day we would be lent out to go and help another farmer if he was short handed. I used to help to fork sheaves of corn or carry corn or clean out the chaff hole or cut bands with Mary and a lass from the village. She kept four cats and would pop the live mice down her jumper. I have seen her catch up to 30 mice and have them running around her middle, held in by a strap. She took them home for the cats. Where she stored them, nobody knows.

Talking about cats, we had a chap who used to go round the farms castrating the cats. If this hadn't been done they would have been overrun. I used to help to round up these cats. The method he used was quite simple. He would place the cats head first into his wellies and then take out his knife! It was over in a flash. He would put some sort of antiseptic on the cat and then let it off. I was only a boy at the time and I thought that was what everybody did to control cats. I know now that it was not the right thing to do, but that is what they did in those days to keep down the cat population. There was always an abundance of cats. Some had diseases and had to be put down. When you think we sometimes had up to 35 to 40 cats running around the place. It was one way I suppose of getting rid of the surplus. I was also learning how to shoot rabbits, etc. They were also available in great numbers and a lot of people were eating them because of the shortage of food. I used to keep my mother supplied with one or two during the war years, which were pretty tough on families for food. We were glad of a couple of rabbits, pheasants or pigeons, etc. Food and sweet rationing was still in force almost until the 50s. It was hard on my parents and others. Most families kept a pig or hens to help out. There was nothing wasted. Even the head was boiled down for potted meat and black pudding. Everybody was good to each other. It's a bit different today. Sometimes you don't know who your neighbours are, but that's life in the town.

I remember us moving to the West End of Darlington because of my son's schooling at Raventhorpe. One lady, when she heard that we were moving to Coniscliffe Road, said "That's where they have lace curtains and kippers!" "You don't say!" I said. I was not too keen on lace curtains, but I was very keen on kippers. It just goes to show what people think about you when you move for the better. We have lace curtains and occasionally kippers. She could have been right.

Sometimes, you know, when I have my breakfast on a morning I have to smile because the chair that I sit on came from Bishop Auckland. Yes - you've guessed it - another boarding up job. This time a very large broken window in Newgate Street. It was between 11.30 pm and 1.30 am. There was nobody about when I arrived and I started to board up. The boards were 8' x 4' and the window was 9' from the pavement so I was just short to reach the top. The pickup was parked around the corner. I had a few yards to walk with the boards, so I thought I would go through the broken window and have a look to see if there were any steps. The only thing I could find to stand on was a chair, which I carried out through the window. It was at that moment that a policeman appeared in front of me and said "I've got you for pinching the chair!" I explained that I couldn't reach the window and that I was going to use it to stand on so that I could knock the nails in, but he didn't believe me and even blamed me for knocking the window out! He got out his notebook and proceeded to ask me my name. I said that my name was on the pickup round the corner. He still did not believe me and demanded my name and address, so I told him I was from Darlington and that the police from Bishop Auckland had called me out. By this time two other policemen came by and asked me if I could manage. They knew me, but this bobby had only been on the beat a few days and thought he had made his first arrest. He was very apologetic and said he was sorry. I told him I would mention the incident to Superintendent Sayers as he was a member of the same golf club as I was, but I was only pulling his leg. After I had boarded up the window, I said to the constable "What are we going to do about the chair? We can't leave it here. If we do then someone will just throw it through another window!" By this time he was getting worried, so I suggested to him that I take it with me for the time being and if he wanted it back he knew where it was. That is how I came to get the chair and still have it even to this day! I use it at breakfast time every morning.

It wasn't long before I was back in Bishop Auckland to board up another window. This time it was an aluminium framed window in Front Street. It had just been put in a few days earlier and was brand new. The Assistant Manager was there and he asked me how I was going to manage to board up the window. I didn't have any 2" x 2" in the pickup. I said I would have to go all the way back to Darlington to get the 2" x 2" to frame it out. That would take me over one hour to get back and as it was around 1.30 in the morning he asked what else could be done. I told him I had some Hilty nails, which would go straight through the aluminium, but would leave a fine hole, or I could go back and load up with timber. I put the decision in his court, I knew he was wanting to get home and so did I. After all I needed my sleep. So he agreed to the Hilty nails and I fitted two 8' x 4' boards in next to no time and back home I went. The following morning I had to ring the Manager regarding the window. He wanted the glass in, but he also wanted a new frame. I went to see him immediately and he gave me a right ticking off and asked my why I had nailed through his aluminium window. I told him that I had discussed it with his Assistant Manager and that after a lot of deliberation he said I could use the Hilty nails. He sent for him and I will say that he took the blame and said that it was not my fault, but I did say that I had some aluminium filler, which I could use to fill the holes up. After a long time he agreed, but he was not a happy man. I was very reluctant to use the Hilty nails again and always made sure that I had plenty of 2" x 2" on the pickup. I boarded that window up once or twice more using 2" x 2" to frame it out.

I remember once in December it had been snowing heavily for two days. I was called out to a shop in Northgate. A large window had been broken and the Manager's son offered to help me by holding the boards etc. We had no sooner started to board up, when there was a loud crack just like thunder and an avalanche of snow fell from the roof. I shouted to the lad to stand close to the window, but he just stayed where he was. The snow came down on him and was up past his knees. He was very scared and shouted for his father. When he saw his son trapped by the snow he dashed inside for a shovel. I was not really worried about the lad, he was still standing up. What worried me more than anything was the fact that my nail box was buried under all that snow. When the Manager brought the shovel I said to him "our priority is the nail box!" I did not want to get them all rusty. It was bad enough having to straighten them without having to use a wire brush on them. So that was what we did - we rescued the nails first! We dug the boy out, but after his experience he no longer wanted to know about 'boarding up'!

I continued to be called out most nights, sometimes fire calls. I remember an occasion when one fireman was left behind by his crew. It all started one evening at around 10 p.m. when a house caught fire. The fire caused considerable damage to the house and the occupant who was a very old lady was badly burned. The fire brigade were called out and after the fire was put out the police sent for me. What a mess it was - windows and doors burnt to a cinder. I started to board up at the back of the house and after I had finished at the back I went around to the front of the house. The policeman was still with me and the fire engine was just leaving. I finished boarding up the front of the house and fitted a second hand door to the front frame. I was just gathering up my tools and the policeman had just gone when I heard a banging noise from inside the house and a voice said "Let me out!" By this time I was a bit worried because the firemen and the police had all gone and there was only me left. He said he was a fireman, but I would not believe him. I said, "show me your axe". He informed me that he did not have one, just a torch. I said I could not let him out as I had done my job and was going home. He got very excited and started to blow his top. I wanted to know who was going to pay for taking the board off the window, after all it was extra work. This sent him into even further rage, but you can understand my position, it was bad enough having to board up without having to take them off again. I told him he would have to go back where he came from and drop through one of the attic trap doors. I knew there were quite a few of these as we had maintained the houses for the Estate Agent for years. I said I would knock at one of the doors and tell them that a fireman wanted to drop in through their bathroom. He did not want to know about that suggestion and after a long talk I decided to take off the board and let him out. As soon as he got through the window he ran like the devil up the street. I shouted at him "You won't catch the fire engine because it left here an hour ago!" I don't think he would ever go poking about in the attics again without someone knowing he was there. I can understand why he didn't want to go through the attics, because they were open in those days and it was a fire hazard. He was looking for sparks and you can imagine what the people would say if they had a fireman dropping into their bathroom. That is where the attic hatches were in some houses. Some did not have any trap door. The houses have since been pulled down and made into units.

Article from the D & S Times
Worth a Scoop

New reporters here are always keen to get to know their Darlington councillors in the hope of future scoops. But an introduction last week to veteran builder and Tory member Councillor Bill Stenson was unusual to say the least. The scene is the D & S Times office at about 10.30 p.m. Two journalists are putting the finishing touches to the last wedding reports of the evening.

Then a kerbstone comes flying through one of the huge Priestgate windows. The two lads jump up and out and join a chap from the Northern Echo on the trail of the alleged vandals. They follow them into a nearby pub, keep an eye on them until the police arrive ...... and then go back to the office for more gypsophila and bridesmaids. But then there's another knock from the same smashed window. Incredulous, they look out only to find Councillor Stenson, who doubles as the town's emergency call-out man, already on the scene with his glue gun and sticky tape. "Alright lads, come out and give us a hand will you", says our Bill, and the pair duly did.

So at 11.30 p.m., after a 14 hour day, they could be seen holding the glass and unpeeling the tape to help Mr. Stenson earn his fiver.

Now that has to be worth a few scoops.

Mr. Fixit

Which brings us on to another Councillor Stenson story.

He's been one of the town's late-night fixers for more than 25 years. Even his mayoral year didn't stop him rushing out to apply glazing first aid to the town's troublespots. On one notable occasion a window was broken late at night at Bishop Auckland Railway Station. The Worshipful Councillor Bill Stenson arrived on the scene still in his finest dinner jacket and set about the repairs as normal. Two men walked past and one was heard to say "I could have sworn that was the Mayor of Darlington in there repairing a window".

"Don't be so daft, I've just seen him at an official function", retorts the friend.

I will now go on to relate another true story which involved a large Chestnut tree in the middle of a potential building site. They had planning permission to build a house, but there was one snag. There was a great tree in the middle of the site. The kids had for the last 100 years been picking conkers off this tree from the day it produced conkers so you know how popular this tree was. A man had heard about me boarding up in the middle of the night and came to see me. He asked me if I would fell this tree in the middle of the night. It could not be done during the day because of the villagers. He said he would pay well. I said I would have to think about it, which I did. I spoke to a specialist woodcutter and he said he would do it as long as we were in the right i.e. planning permission etc., and that the restrictions on the tree had been lifted.

He said "No problem", and the woodcutter went and did the job in the middle of the night. Some residents were woken up by the power saw, but we were lucky to escape the wrath of the people. The job was done and the Darlington & Stockton Times that Saturday had an article about the chestnut tree with the headlines "Villagers Hunt Phantom Woodcutter".

It has not been an easy job boarding up especially in the winter months with frost, snow and ice on the roads. Driving conditions were pretty dicey for me and my man Stanley. Stanley was a godsend to me and I am sure that he has one or two tales to tell, from the time he worked for me. I will ask him one of these days. I remember one New Year's Eve we had a few friends in for supper and to "First Foot" in other words to let in the New Year. It was while we were having our cake and sherry that I got a phone call from the police to a pub in Butterknowle. The pickup heater had gone and was not working, it was just blowing cold air.

It was snowing and frosty and the roads were bad. I thought I might take one of the guests with me so I asked for volunteers and Horace, a friend of ours, said he would like to go and find out what I did on these call outs. I told him that the heater was not working and that it would be a cold journey to the pub. His daughter Pat said that he would be alright, he was well clothed with Trilby and coat and off we went. By the time we had gone a few miles he was freezing and feeling the cold and so was I. The pickup glass was freezing up and I was having a job keeping the windscreen clean. I was getting concerned about Horace who was in his late seventies.

Eventually we arrived at the pub and I went straight in to enquire about the window and also to see if Horace could get thawed out. The landlord said bring him in. We took him in to the crowded pub and sat him down next to the big roaring fire and plied him with whiskey and other drinks. The pub was quite busy and I boarded up the window and asked the landlord if I could fit the glass in two days time.

I went to get Horace out of the pub. By this time he was not only warm, but was getting quite drunk. I said to the Landlord that it was very cold outside and my fingers were nearly frozen off. I thought he might have given me a drink. Not him - he said I was driving and I should not drink but I am sure a little tipple would not have hurt me. With a great effort I got Horace out of the pub and into the pickup and set off home. The amount of alcohol Horace had consumed kept him warm on the way home and the smell of his breath helped me to keep me warm!

When we got home I got into trouble off Laura for taking Horace, but Horace enjoyed it! So another New Year's Eve was spoilt and it is only very rarely that I stay in to celebrate Christmas or New Year. I felt that I would be letting down the business people of our town and also the public and I have some stories to tell about them. I remember going to a house on a council estate one night after midnight to board up the lounge window. The husband had knocked his wife about and really hurt her and when I got there the man was fast asleep on the settee and the woman said let the blighter sleep. I boarded up the window and as I was walking through the lounge he woke up and he thought I was after his wife. It took me quite a while to calm him down. It was just as well I had my hammer in my pocket which seemed to calm him, but he was still drunk and it made me wonder what I am doing in this job with all its perils and hassles, but the good people you meet make up for the bad.

Right: The businessman. Me as
we were building up our
business
Below: Loyal servant. Our first
pickup!

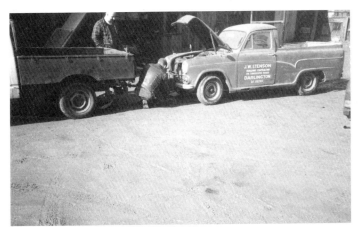

CHAPTER SIX

Around about this time I was still building houses etc. I have two stories to tell about the site where we were building. We would dig a large 5' hole in the ground and place a little tin hut for the men's toilet uses. This consisted of two stakes driven into the ground and then a piece of 4" x 2" nailed across it so that they could sit on it. When we dug this pit it rained overnight and filled up with water.

One of the labourers went to use it next day and he always tried to skive a few minutes reading the papers. When I asked where he was they said he had gone to the loo so I got hold of a quarter brick and threw it on the roof. You can just imagine the sound of that brick hitting the tin shed roof. He got such a shock that he fell off the seat and into the water. He yelled and started to swear. We got him out, but he was in such a state of shock he had to go home and change. It was a good job he was the first to use it and it got a good christening. He reported me to Laura when he picked up his wages and my defence was that he was spending too much time in the loo and I only did it for fun. He soon saw the funny side of it and he did not lose any pay for having the day off.

Not all things end like that. On the same site I used to leave my wellies in the shed that we used for materials and one morning it started to rain. We were working on the foundations laying bricks and I needed my wellies on. Employers in those days did not supply employees with wellingtons. You had to supply your own. When I got to the site a bit later one of the brickies got hold of my wellies and would not take them off. A row developed and it got quite nasty. He said they were his wellies even though my name was inside them. I said he would have to take them off and he lost his temper and aimed at my head with a 3' level. I ducked and it hit me on the shoulder. That was when I saw red and let go with my fist and hit him under the chin and knocked him into a barrow. He lay there, but unknown to me a lady upstairs had seen me hit him, but did not see him hit me first with the level, but my foreman joiner had. Unbeknown to me she sent for the police, but by this time the bricklayer had come round and was sorry he had caused all the fuss when he realised the wellingtons were mine.

Anyway the bobby arrived and told me that the lady had seen me hit him, but had not seen him hitting me first with the level. She had drawn the curtains just in time to see me hit him and it was a case of seeing only part of what had happened and when the policeman explained this to her she came round and apologised to me. I think she learned a lesson from this and so did I. I kept my wellies in the pick-up from then on. If that incident had been serious, I was the prime suspect, which makes you think about other similar cases.

I continued to build village halls at the rate of nearly one a year and church halls and did stonework on churches etc. which I enjoyed immensely and I received one of the best awards for craftsmanship for stonework. My spare time in those days was spent playing golf with my son who was a very good golfer, also cricket, snooker, etc. when I had the time.

I remember one night Laura asked if I would I bring some fish and chips home for supper. Our supper in those days was around about 10.30 in the evening. Tom, my friend at that time, thought he would take some home for his wife as well. We both lived in the West End of the town and I said I would go in to the fish shop and get them while he sat outside and looked after the pickup which was loaded with 8' x 4' ply. After about ten minutes I got back into the pickup and drove off. I had not gone very far - about 200 yards, when I saw this man carrying an 8' x 4' board up the street. I said to Tom, that's my board and I pulled up alongside the man and said "that's my board" expecting him to drop it and run, but not him! He started to argue that it was his and was just taking it home. I told him it was my board and that I could prove it by the nail holes in it and I would be calling the police. He said he did not want an 8'x 4' board with nail holes in it and he dropped it and ran up the street. Tom had dozed off and had not heard a thing while he was sitting in the pickup. He never heard the last of that incident and we never went for fish and chips again at night. I learnt a lesson and from then on I always fastened the boards down with a rope to keep them safe.

After that a friend of mine was always asking that I ring him up if I was called out in the middle of the night. One night I got a call and rang him and told him I would pick him up in ten minutes. Sure enough there he was standing with his hammer ready to go. Denis was very pleased and wanted to come out on other evenings, which he did on occasions when he answered the phone. This particular night we were called out to Newton Aycliffe. On the top floor about three or four windows had been broken and Denis said I should drive up the walkway so we would not have so far to carry the boards and up we went and on to the landing to board up the windows. This was a very difficult job and it took us more time to get that pickup down from the first floor of the town centre than it did going there and boarding up. Never again did I do that and Denis got a right ticking off. You learn from your mistakes!

It is only fair that people want to know how much you charge for boarding up. I remember one night I was called out as someone had broken into the Synagogue in Tower Road which belonged to the Jews of our town, who are very nice people, but when it comes down to business they are 'spot on'! It was a lesson that I learned to be thrifty.

When I got there the fire had been put out and they were waiting for me to arrive to board up. They would not let me board up until I had given them a price and after a lot of arguments I gave them a price and they said they would have to discuss it with the elders. They all went into a huddle and then came back and said I was too high. I said I was right about the price and would not come down. They went into a huddle again and came and asked for discount. I stuck to my guns and I said that if they did not agree the price soon, I would have to raise the price because of the time spent arguing. I was just wasting my time and if they did not agree I would be going home and leaving it to them. They all agreed and I boarded up and the next day I put the glass in, but what a hard life just to earn a crust of bread.

CHAPTER SEVEN

Tom and I were discussing one night in the club that we might like to grow our own vegetables. I thought it was a very good idea so I wrote to the Council about the allotments in the west end of the town where we both lived. Sure enough after a week or two they said I could have one which had become vacant. I fixed up a time with Tom so we could go and see where it was and if it was alright. We arranged a time convenient to both of us and set off to view it. We were both excited about this new venture. Well, it had rained all day and when we got there we could not find it. The number of the allotment was at the bottom of the site and it was flooded. According to the plan the site was right in the middle of the flood! You can imagine what Tom and I thought about the Council allotments. I said "Leave this to me Tom, I will write them a serious letter", which I did. In my letter I told them that we had looked at the site and it was flooded. No way could we accept the allotment to grow vegetables on it. We were not Chinamen and we did not want to grow rice as the place was a paddy field. I asked them to look at our application again.

Someone from the Town Hall sent my letter around the Parks Department and after three weeks or more another allotment became vacant. Off we went again - same site but different number. When we got there and saw the number of trees on the site we could not believe our eyes. There were apple trees, plum trees, pear trees and also flowering shrubs. Tom was aghast, there was no room to grow any vegetables. By this time I was beginning to lose my cool with the Council. You would think we had done something to them. The pair of us were honourable citizens and I was even on the Council and on the allotment sub-committee. We had done everything legal by putting our names down on their list. Back to the pen and paper and in no uncertain terms, I told them what I thought about them. As I was not a lumberjack and had no intention of starting up a business in timber, I told them that we did not want this allotment and to please take our names off the list. I did not hear from them again - typical council.

It was weeks later that I was working on a church in the town when a man said that he had heard about my plight regarding the allotments. He said that he was going to Scotland to work and would be leaving the area in two to three weeks and if we paid him for all the stuff that he had planted then we could have it. Incidentally it was on the same site as the ones we had seen. The cost being £10 - £5 each. So I put it to Tom: now, Tom being a Scotsman said "How do we know he has planted the seeds - potatoes etc?" Doubting Thomas you see! I said we would have to take his word for it, but no, Tom wanted to be sure, so off we went to view it. Sure enough it was all set and Tom poked about to see if he could find the potatoes as they hadn't come through the ground as they had just been planted. So we paid the man £10 and he said he would have to give notice to the Council, but would give them our names. I also rang them and much to my surprise they gave us permission to stay on.

We stayed on for two years and then packed it up. What a saga just to get one allotment from the Council. I brought it up at the allotment sub- committee and of course the press got hold of it. I only hope other people don't have such bad luck. The allotment we were first given has now ended up as part of the car park.

We still kept on boarding up and re-glazing windows and still incidents kept on happening to me. I used to board up the Rugby Club every two weeks and it was always in the middle of the night and the cigarette machines and fruit machines were the target. I take my hat off to the Secretary of that club who took it all in his stride after all we were losing quite a bit of sleep and it always involved one or two hours depending how many windows there were. Coming back from the Rugby Club one night, going round the roundabout was a big dog fox. He set off down Yarm Road with me following him all the way till we got to the centre of the town, then he went on to the centre and to this day we still have foxes in our town who roam about the streets scavenging for food.

This job boarding up does not always have the stories to tell that I have previously told. It also has its drawbacks. I have been lamed a few times over the past years working up a height and on scaffolding and when the scaffolder forgot to fasten one of the pudlicks I was working on with one of my apprentices, the whole lot collapsed and we fell from about 28'. I passed the apprentice going down. We were hit by planks of wood and also the steel scaffolding. We both landed on our feet and I broke a bone on the vertebrae. In other words I broke my neck and I was off work for some time. We were very lucky to be alive. The apprentice left and joined the Army, saying he would sooner risk getting shot as fall down from that scaffolding again. I sacked the guy who fixed the scaffolding. This accident put me out of action for quite a while in the late 70s. It took place at a farmhouse in the country and during this time our yard was at King William Street and that's when we bought out Will Hirstwood, who was one of the local undertakers. We stayed there for a few years then we built up the site which is now Kay Grove, which was a nice development of flats and houses. Then in 1967 we bought McKenzie's business at 52 Duke Street where we still are now and where we have been involved building houses, factories etc. and still boarding up.

This leads me on to another true story about a fireman. I was called out to a fire on one of the trading estates where we had a number of windows to board up and I took one of my joiners to board up with. When we got there the fire brigade were still there and they would not let me board up till they were sure that the fire was out. After one hour standing about I said to the officer in charge that I wanted to get home and back to bed for my sleep.

He reluctantly said "You can board up now." So we started to cut the boards and frame out the windows because they were steel. We nailed up quite a lot of windows and left only one which had a hose pipe sticking through it and I said to the joiner the fire brigade must have left their hose pipe, so I started to pull it out of the window. Much to my surprise and the joiners there was a fireman on the end of it. I nearly had a fit for the amount of abuse that he gave me was nobody's business. He said that there were still some sparks in the building and that was why he wanted the hose. It appeared to me that it was still connected to the water hydrant and the building at the far end was still on fire and I had to wait until the 'all clear' was given by his Chief. Yet unknown to us the fire engine and crew were at the other end of the building and I had had a belly full of firemen. After all, we had already had the earlier fiasco with a fireman! After 1 am we were able to board up that window. I was never in a hurry to go to fires because of the time wasted.

I recall going to Crook one night around about 2 am when one of the job centres had been damaged. One window and one door had been broken. People are very kind in the middle of the night and the Manager gave me a hand. And while I was boarding up the job centre I was just about finished when a man who was going to work said "By lad, what are you doing?" and I said "Can't you see, I've boarded up the Job Centre". He then said I should be ashamed of myself for boarding up the Job Centre in the middle of the night. Then he said "How many have you boarded up tonight?" I told him "Three!" and he said "That bloody Margaret Thatcher has something to answer for. You did not expect me to see you boarding up the centre and I will have something to say about this when I get to work!"

That same night I did board up three premises one at Barnard Castle, which was a shop window and one at Darlington. But he thought I had boarded up three Job Centres and it was when the Conservatives were in power and Mrs Thatcher was closing Job Centres down all over the country. No wonder the man from Crook was worried when I told him I had boarded up those three: he thought that I had actually closed them down and was going around the towns closing down the job centres on orders from Mrs Thatcher.

One Saturday night there was a thunderstorm at about 10pm. The storm was very bad and the town was very busy at that time with youngsters going to the discos and pubs etc. All of a sudden the heavens opened and the rain came pelting down and there was a terrific crash of thunder, which the people said was a thunderbolt. It hit a very high chimney on Lloyds Bank and brought it crashing down onto the pavement below. But because the rain was so torrential, all the youngsters who were walking along that way had taken cover out of the rain and consequently no-one was hurt. There was approximately two tons or more of debris, which had fallen into the street.

When I got there my job was to move all the debris off the street and take it back to our yard. Then we had to bring several extension ladders and I had to call out two of my men and examine the chimney to make sure there was nothing loose that would come down on to the street. With the help of the police we cordoned it off. On the Monday morning we had to erect a scaffold on the front of the bank to make sure that the chimney was safe and also to make templates of the stone which had come off and which were now lying in my yard.

During the time that we put up the scaffold and we were working on one part of the chimney to secure it, a brick fell down onto the pavement below. At the same time as the brick fell there was a man walking underneath the scaffold. The brick came down and took all the buttons off his shirt. He had no other damage apart from the buttons off his shirt and the shock!

I nipped down smartish from the top of the scaffold, which would be about 40' at least, when I heard him shouting and then he said "Wasn't I lucky! I have worked in the building trade all my life and I know that accidents like this can happen, but I didn't think I could escape with only the buttons off my shirt."

I said I would buy him a new shirt and he said that was all he wanted. "If you can provide me with that I will be very grateful." I took his size and asked him to call in at the office and Laura would buy him a new shirt. Which she did. He came to our office in Duke Street and Laura gave him his Double Two shirt with the price ticket still on. He said he had never had such an expensive shirt.

To this day I don't know how the brick got through, as we had safety netting all around the scaffolding. I think both he and I were very lucky that day!

CHAPTER EIGHT

The case of the missing saw: Stanley and I were sent to board up the premises of a local restaurant on Northgate which had been on fire and we arrived after the firemen had gone and we started to board up the place. Stanley was cutting the boards and I was nailing them on to the frames. The owner and his son were also there. Stanley put the saw down and went to get another 8' x 4' board off the pickup. He went to pick up his saw and low and behold he could not find it. There were no people about except the four of us and I had not taken it and I don't think the owner had taken it, or his son. The owner was a policeman and said he had not seen it. So where was the saw? Stanley was really worried. This had not happened before on any of our board up jobs. We looked high and low, but to no avail.

We didn't have a spare one and I said to Stanley, "What are you going to do now?" Well he said "that's a mystery!" and so it was. There was nobody about. Where had the saw gone? We haven't got time to get another one from home. You will have to cut it with a chisel. It was a good job we only needed one more board. That saw never turned up yet! Next day I had to buy a new saw. It is rather strange that we had a policeman on the job and yet that saw disappeared. Where it went to nobody knows. I think that someone who was passing during that time had taken that saw when Stanley had put it down and was not looking.

The next story I would like to tell relates to a board up at a shop, which was empty in one of the Council estates. I had an accident on this job on a very slippery yard when the ladder slipped and I fell 18' to the ground and lamed my legs and chest and sprained both ankles and my hands which put me out of work for some weeks. I could hardly walk without the stick. So Stanley was quite busy doing the call outs until one night he could not go and I said to the police that I would come and as it was just a kitchen window which had two panes broken I said I would be alright and off I went. When I got there, this policeman was standing there and he showed me the broken window at the house. I quickly boarded up the kitchen window. He then said what about the yard door. We will have to make it safe. I said that because of my ankle and legs I would not be able to climb over the wall after I had put the boards in and I said to him, "you will have to do it!" He said he would not do it because it was not his job. I had to do some quick thinking then. So I said "The Sergeant said you would do it". I know I was telling a little white lie, but because of my legs it was not possible for me to do it. So he reluctantly said he would do it. Over the wall he went and he tried to get the door shut.

After a while he managed to shut it by using his foot, but by then he could not get the bolts in because they were so stiff. He had taken off his helmet and it was laid on the ground near me outside the back door until he had jumped over the wall. He started shouting, he could not get the bolts in and would I throw him the hammer, which I did. There was such a yell. The hammer had hit him on the head and really hurt him and it was my heavy claw hammer. He did eventually get the bolts in after a lot of shouting and then he jumped over the wall after he had thrown the hammer over and I stood clear so the same thing did not happen to me. When he got down from the wall the first thing he said was that he would have to report it to the Sergeant. I said "If you have to then do so, but it wouldn't look right to tell him that I had hit you with the hammer when you were at that side of the wall and I was at this side. It wouldn't be very convincing would it?" and I said it was an accident. He soon saw the funny side and I said to him that I was sorry about the accident. By then the van came and picked him up and I don't think he ever said a word about it. I went home and he went back to the Police Station and Stan was still helping me out in the middle of the night until I was well enough to carry on.

CHAPTER NINE

A lady from Hercules Street called in to see me at the office at 12.30 one day. It was my usual custom to have a sandwich and a cup of coffee with Laura at the office at this time each day. However, on this particular day I was tied up elsewhere and did not go back to the office. Laura informed the lady that I was not coming back that day. She would not tell Laura her problem and said she would call back later. Sure enough she did, but it was three years later. Once again she called at the same time of day and asked if I was in and Laura had to say that I was not and would not be in until 4.30 p.m. as I was working out of town. Again she said she would call back to see me. She would not give her address and nobody would believe this except for our own staff in the office. She did call again at exactly the same time of day and this time she found me eating my sandwiches. This was approximately seven years after her first visit and she told me what her problem was and asked if I would be able to help her. She had had no water from any of her taps in the house and would I go and see what the trouble was. She had read about me helping people over the last few years in the local newspapers in my job as a Councillor and would I be able to help. I said I would try and that if she went straight home I would be with her in 30 minutes and I would bring David Walker with me, the plumber who was doing work for us on a regular basis. I rang David and he said he would be ready if I picked him up around 1 p.m. I was becoming very interested in the fact that this lady had had no water for seven years. How had she been managing? David and I set off with a pick, a shovel and plumbing tools to test the water supply. When we got there we found that the lady was right - she had no water. We decided to dig down to the stopcock, which was in the yard and approximately 2' deep. When we took the top off the stopcock there was not a drop of water. It was as dry as a bone. We came to the conclusion that the supply pipe had been cut off for the last few years. I said that I would have to ring the Water Board and get them up pronto.

This is where the problems started. I got on to the water board and spoke to an engineer and explained that the lady in question had not had any drinking water for the last seven years and would he come up and see for himself while we were still there at the house? He said that he could not come that day, but I said "you must come to see it immediately as it is your problem now." He hummed and hahed and I threatened to go to the newspaper, as this was the kind of story that they liked. As soon as I mentioned newspapers he said he would be with me in about thirty minutes and I thanked him. David and I waited and true to his word he was on time. When he saw that the pipe and the stopcock had no water, he could not believe it. I said that I thought that the water pipe had been cut off in the back lane at some time in the past. No, he did not agree. He got on to his mobile and sent for somebody else in authority. By this time the lady was telling him that she had had no water for the last seven years. She had been collecting rainwater from the roof to do her washing and flush the manhole because her toilet had been broken by the builder next door. He had been doing repairs and had dropped a brick through the roof and broken the outside toilet, which was the only one she had. She had a commode that she used upstairs at night and then flushed away down the manhole with the rainwater. The manhole cover she had to lift was not light especially for a lady in her eighties. You can imagine her struggling with the top. She told me she used a screwdriver and a chisel to get the top off. The handles had rusted off in the middle of the manhole cover.

The next man and woman arrived from the Water Board to view the pipe and said that it was not their fault and that the water had not been cut off. They were trying to pass the buck. I said if they did not do something by tomorrow to get this lady's water on - I would bring in the TV and the national newspapers. They had a little meeting together to discuss it while David and I waited for their deliberation. After a long discussion they said they would dig up the back lane in the morning. I thanked them and said I would see them in the morning. I told the lady in question what was happening and that she would have water in the next 24 hours. She was very pleased. Next day I was there to see if I was right about the water pipe having been cut off by the Water Board or someone else.

They arrived after 9 am and the workmen started digging with a JCB and to no surprise of mine or David's the lead pipe had been cut off for the last seven years. They sent for the guy who did not believe that the pipe had been cut off. By this time he had gone and was nowhere to be seen, but he had to come back. When he arrived he apologised to both to me and the lady and I said "What are you going to do about it?" Well he looked me straight in the eye and said "What do you think?" I said "Get the water on - get new pipe in!" They dug the trench for a new pipe from the back lane to the house and the only thing David and I had to do was connect the pipe up to the sink in the small kitchen. She only had one kitchen sink and one bath and one hot water cylinder. No washbasin in the bathroom which was downstairs and the water cylinder was not working. Over the seven years without water, it had rusted up consequently the water cylinder was no good. So we had to stop the water from getting to the cylinder and cut that off.

The lady was very reluctant to use the tap at first. She seemed scared of the amount of water coming out. After all she'd had lead pipes over the last 80 years which were not running at full bore. She told me she had been buying water when she could afford it and when she could not she got it out of the ladies toilets in the market by placing a bottle under the cold water tap, filling a gallon or two and then coming home. She bought some water at the supermarket near to her home. I really admired this lady. She was so proud not to complain and I blame myself for not being in the office when she first came to see me years ago, as I always went to the office at that time of day. The sad part about it was she would not give her address or any information to Laura or to Joyce who were in the office. She would not phone me as she was a bit hard of hearing and had no phone in the house. It must have been fate.

After the water was on the next job I had to do for her was to try and get her Water and Sewerage Rates back. She had regularly paid her rates every year and that is where the fun started again.

There was a bit of a twist to this true story. The lady in question had two brothers who died within a week of each other. Her house was in bad need of repair and she could not afford to have a new sink unit, window, etc. the roof repairs, new gutters, also a new toilet in the bathroom, nor could she afford to paint the house and she also wanted tiling and pointing doing. That is where the brothers came in - they left her a sum of money. How much I do not know. When she came back after attending the funerals down south. She got in touch with me and asked me to do all the jobs that would brighten up her life. She had no television. When we bought a new TV at Christmas, Laura offered her a black and white one that we had, which was in good working order. What I admired about this lady was her cleanliness. Her house was immaculately clean, yet she had had no water, but was clean and independent. We did all the work except the new bath. She would not have a new bath as the cast iron bath, which had been fitted when the house was built, was in good condition. It is now just a year or two since this lady died. She did not live long enough to enjoy the money that her brothers left to her. I was only too pleased to have known her. What a lady to live without water for seven years, expecting that water to come on at any time! I was pleased to get some of the money back i.e. the water rates etc.

The papers never got hold of this story because she did not want the publicity and I, as a local Councillor respected her wishes.

CHAPTER TEN

I have not mentioned anything about the Council - this could come as a sequel to this book, if I so wish. After all it is a long time to serve the community - 37 years and still serving and also being mayor of the Borough of Darlington in 1981/82. I will tell you of one classic story of when I was mayor which is true. It could only happen to me as a builder.

I used to visit the Mayor's Charity Shop regularly. The shop was short of space and had a fireplace at the back of the shop where they stored all the clothes that had to be sorted and hung on to rails. Being a charitable chap I said to Mrs Hutchinson that I would take out the fireplace and brick it up so they would have a flat wall where they could put a rail to hang some of the clothes.

One Saturday morning I set off with a barrow full of bricks, sand and cement to brick up the fireplace. I had my working clothes on which included a tattered old jacket, which I took off and hung on the back of the door in the charity shop. Unknown to me the shop was open and people were coming in and out and trying things on. All of a sudden my jacket had disappeared from the back of the door. This chap had picked it up to try it on. Then he saw the holes in the sleeve and said to Mrs Hutchinson "The Charity Shop must be in a terrible state selling rubbish like this". Mrs. Hutchinson said to him "Will you take that jacket off, it belongs to the mayor." I came through and saw this chap wearing my jacket. I said "Get that ruddy jacket off - it's mine". Mrs. Hutchinson said "This is the mayor". The chap then said "I didn't know you were in such a bad state as that. I would have brought some jackets in." I took my jacket off him and kept it with me where I was bricking up the fireplace. Mrs Hutchinson was rather amused and told that true story on many occasions. Laura destroyed the jacket when she heard about it and said I should be ashamed of myself, especially as I was the mayor of Darlington.

I remember very well the day I had to relinquish my office as mayor. On the night before, I installed the new mayor with all the pomp and ceremony that goes with it and I was left to find my own way home, because I had no chauffeur and no car. I just felt dejected, because the mayor's chauffeur was looking after the new mayor and rightly so. I was feeling a little bit sad. It had been a bad winter and it was now spring and I had a big job to do next morning with my men and I was looking forward to it. I did not take any money from the council ie attendance allowances. I was allocated the mayor's allowance, which I used to entertain visitors and guests. I was glad to get back to work to earn a bob or two and this is where the story begins in Barclays' entrance off Skinnergate. Friday morning just after I had been mayor I was taking up concrete and tarmac which had to be replaced with 6" of concrete.

There I was helping the lads to break up the concrete and load it on to our three ton wagon. I was using a pick hammer and shovel when two gentleman coming along Skinnergate said to me "Weren't you the mayor yesterday?" and what was the Council doing putting me on a job like this picking and shovelling and breaking up concrete. "Its not on!" one of them said. "You weren't a bad mayor and the council should have given you a better job than this." I said to them "I rather like doing this work. It keeps me fit" and they shook their heads and said it was terrible, the council officials want their heads looking at. I couldn't help but smile. So I said to them that I was very lucky that the council had given me this job to do because I knew what was going to happen to the new mayor and they said "What?" and I said "You will have to keep what I am telling you secret". They said they would not breath a word and then I told them that the council were going to send him to Siberia. I said "This is so", and one of them said you have been lucky and I said I am very grateful to the Council for giving me this job. It just goes to show that the people in our town don't know what goes on. They went on their way shaking their heads and I got on with my job. My lads were amazed that people were worried about what happens to past mayors.

We still continued to board up in the borough and fit the glass. Strange things happen when you are boarding up shop windows. People often stop and ask for items from the window. If it is a shoe shop, they want a pair of shoes. They even tell us the size and we tell them to "Get Lost!" or words to that effect. People think that because the window is broken they can help themselves. We have also had one or two of our tools stolen hammers and saws etc. They also want to help you hit the nails into the board and also use the saw. I have to tell them that they can't have them and that is when they can get a bit nasty especially when they have had too much to drink. They think they are good joiners who only want to help by using the hammer and saw and knocking the nails in. It is my policy never to leave go of the hammer or saw, because the general public can be very aggressive when they've had too much to drink. Little do they know that glass is a serious hazard and not for playing around with.

I can remember one night a lady who was wearing stiletto heeled shoes broke some windows by taking off her shoe and knocking out the door panes as she ran down the street, before the police got hold of her. It was drink that caused her to do this. Stanley repaired a few that night. In the 80s it was a regular occurrence - broken windows were happening regularly, Fridays, Saturdays and Sundays in all the towns. As they do today, but not so often because during the 90s and 2000s we have got CCTV cameras. This has certainly reduced crime, by I would say 80% to 90%. Most towns and cities have them now, so we don't get the number of call outs as we did 30 years ago or even five years ago. In a way I welcome the cameras, except that it has done my business a lot of harm, but that's progress. We still continue to board up in 2004 and fit glass etc. These are just some of the events that happened to me while I was on call and working with the police. I have only touched the tip of the iceberg.

On many occasions I have been called out to fix a dining room or lounge window, where a pheasant has flown right through the glass when the sun has been shining and the bird has seen the reflection. They would land on the table or other furnishings and could do quite a bit of damage to the room in question and also break their necks.

During the 80s we owned quite a large house in the west end of the town with planning permission for bungalows, but the house had been converted into flats and these were tenanted.

One of the flats had two occupants when there should have only been one. All the flats were rented in one person's name and they were not supposed to have anyone else living in the flat at all. The occupant owed me rent and would not vacate the flat. He said he was a squatter. The legitimate tenant had told him he could take over the tenancy because he was leaving. That was how this man became a squatter. The rent kept mounting up and still he wouldn't pay, so strict action had to be taken as I was losing too much rent. So one night I called at the flat, but the tenant was not in. He did not know that I had a spare key, so I let myself in and I became the 'squatter'. Well I sat around for some time and put the latch down so he could not get in. When he arrived he tried his key and wondered what was the matter. That was when I opened the window and demanded my rent for the last few weeks, because he was not the proper tenant and he had squatted. I said he could become the new tenant if he paid the rent that he owed. He said no but that he had just got a new cooker in the kitchen and would I let him have it? I said he could have the cooker if he paid me the rent owing and he said he would have to go and borrow some money and he disappeared. I then changed the lock and waited. After about one and a half hours he came back with just half of the money. So I let him have the cooker which he loaded in to the van he had brought back with him and then went on his way and I went home for my supper. That was my taste of being a squatter! It was not a nice experience sitting there in the flat and wondering what was going to happen.

This is where the job of being a landlord gets a bit serious. I was about to go away for my annual summer holiday when I realised I only had 24 hours to get a summons to another tenant because he owed rent. So next morning around 7am I set off to the other side of the town to bring back the bailiff to deliver the summons. Well when I got to the bailiff's house he was still in bed and when he did get up he was not amused and played war with me for waking him and the whole household. I reminded him that he had told me if I knew the tenant was in I could go and get the summons. He said "but it's Saturday!" Anyway after some argument we set off to the flats in my pickup to give the man his summons. I knew he was in because I had gone by that way before I went for the bailiff. When we got to the flat, I had a spare key for the front door, but not for any of the other doors. I opened the front door, but the bedroom door was fastened with a charlie band. The bailiff said "We can't break in to the bedroom!" By this time the tenant was awake and trying to escape out of the bedroom window which would not open. So I put my shoulder against the door and it flew open. To our surprise, the woman was naked and started to shout all sorts of things at us, but I pushed the bailiff into the bedroom, much to his surprise and I said "That's him - Give him the bloody summons". That is how we came to get the tenant out. In those days the bailiff had to place the summons into the hands of the tenant before you could get them to Court. I then took the bailiff home and I went on holiday. After the Court case we got possession of the flat, got a new tenant and we had no more trouble.

I remember well the day that Laura asked me to take the bedroom curtains to be dry cleaned. I put them on the seat in the pickup, but before I took them to the cleaners I was going to a job with Brian, the joiner where we were to hack out and re-glaze a pane of glass and put a new lock on the bedroom door. We were also doing work in the kitchen where he needed a dustsheet. I told Brian to get some dust sheets from the back of the pickup and to put them down before he started the job. He then proceeded to hack out the glass and I left him to get on while I went to the dry cleaners. When I arrived at the cleaners I handed over the curtains and the lady said there was only one curtain. I said "there can't be - I had two when I left home!"

Then it dawned on me what had happened and I hurried back to where Brian was doing the job hoping that no damage had been caused to the curtain! When I arrived, there was our good bedroom curtain spread across the floor and covered with broken glass and wood shavings. I said to Brian, "Do you realise that you have got our best bedroom curtains on the floor! What is Laura going to say if you have damaged them!"

I immediately started to take up the curtain and examine it for damage. As luck would have it, there was no damage and I hastened back to the cleaners with it.

Laura knew nothing of this until she was recently talking to a friend of hers about curtains. I began to laugh as I recalled the episode of the bedroom curtain and I had to come clean and tell her what had happened.

An engineer who I knew rang me up and asked me if I would be interested in a very tricky job at one of the nursing homes in Darlington. I said yes I would go with him and see what the problem was and if possible we would do the job. So he called and picked me up from the office and off we went. When we got there, there was a coach parked outside the home. We went into the foyer and he said "wait there Bill and I'll go and see the matron." He was away quite a time - 10 minutes or more. I was sitting there minding my own business when a lady came dashing through the front door and said "ah there you are -get yourself on that bloody bus we've been waiting for you and look at your clothes you aren't even properly dressed!" I said "I think you have made a mistake, I don't even live here! Anyway where are we going?" She said "On a mystery tour!" I said "Well I'm very sorry, I would like to go on a mystery tour but I'm here to look at the water tanks with an engineer!" By this time the engineer came back and I said "You are lucky to find me here - they've been trying to get me on that ruddy bus!" At this point he said "I've got news for you, we are at the wrong nursing home!" The lady was very apologetic when she realised her mistake. We made a hasty retreat and I can tell you I was very relieved to have escaped! We then went on to the other nursing home which was the right one and I said to Don "I shall stay with you - I don't want the same thing to happen again". We continued to do the job over the next day or two, which proved to be a very tricky job, but we did it nevertheless. I never did find out where they were going!

It has been an eventful life during which I have seen plenty of changes ... and not all for the better, in my view. It seems to me that there was much to recommend the 'old days'. Equally eventful have been my council experiences and there are a lot of stories I could tell. But maybe they will have to wait. Perhaps one day I will tell those stories as well - if I live long enough to write them!

Top: Civic duties. Serving as a Councillor and meeting the Princess Royal during one of her visits to the North East

Bottom: Modern times. Me and workmate Ned Kelly